Edmaz Book of English Language:

Junior Secondary Level

—Revised Edition—

Published

By

Edson Mazira

ISBN 978-1-77906-385-4

Edmaz Book of English Language:

Junior Secondary Level

—Revised Edition—

Preamble

Edmaz Book of English Language: Junior Secondary Level has a package of language structures for secondary school beginners. The book seeks to develop each student's level of understanding and writing English.

At the end, there are answers to all the questions set to test the student.

Acknowledgement

I grab this moment to thank veteran writers from whose books I consumed quality education. These are Shimmer Chinodya, Charles Mungoshi, S.R. Golding, Raymond Murphy, John Hart, Peter Herring, John Eastwood, Jane Straus and many others.

Finally, I thank my brothers Christopher Mazira and Luckson Mazira for their support.

Contents

Chapter one

Nouns

A *noun* is a naming word; its definition is not limited. *Nouns* have categories or types.

The following are some of the categories:

Proper nouns and common nouns

These are the main categories in which all the nouns are bi-classified permanently. *Proper nouns* are the names of people or places; they start with capital letters anywhere they are written: James, Samson, Harare, Zimbabwe, Mukumbura, and so on. It is wrong to start any of these with a small letter: james, samson, harare, zimbabwe, and so on.

Common nouns are common names of things. Almost everything on earth has a common noun, but not everything has a proper noun or name.

Unlike the proper nouns, the common nouns start with small letters anywhere they are written: person, animal, country, sugar, love, and so on. But when we use them to start sentences, they start with capital letters: *Love is sweet.* **S***ugar is also sweet.*

Since we say almost everything on earth has a *common noun,* but not everything has a *proper noun,* the following table proves it:

Proper noun	Common noun
1. James or Lydia	1. person
2. Nil	2. sky
3. Zimbabwe	3. country
4. Nil	4. maize
5. Bindura	5. town
6. Mary	6. girl
7. Nil	7. boxes
8. Nil	8. soil

Subject nouns and object nouns

These are minor categories into which both proper and common nouns are temporarily put according to their positions in any grammatical sentence.

One noun can act as a subject in one sentence and then as an object in another:

1. *Lydia* scolded *James.*
   Subject — verb — *object*
2. *James* scolded *Lydia.*
   Subject — verb — *object*

In number 1, *Lydia* is the *subject* of the sentence, whereas *James* is the *object*.

In number 2, *James* is now the *subject* of the sentence, whereas *Lydia* is the *object*.

The subject of a sentence is known as *the agent of the action.* The subject can be a noun, a pronoun or a phrase or clause acting as a noun.

The object of a sentence is known as *the sufferer of the action.* The object can be a noun, a pronoun or a phrase or clause acting as a noun.

The action in these terms (the agent of *the action* and the sufferer of *the action*) is a verb. A verb is a word that shows action or state of being. It makes us know what action *was, is* or *will be* given to the object by the subject, and it is the root of a grammatical predicate (the whole sentence without the subject).

1. James scolded Lydia.

From this, James is the *subject noun (the agent of the action)*; he is the one who *acted to* Lydia. Lydia is the *object noun (the sufferer of the action)*; she suffered *the action* from James.

Collective nouns

A *collective noun* is a single name given to a group of people or things: *gang*—a *gang* of thieves, *fleet*—a *fleet* of buses, *congregation*—a *congregation* of church members, and so on.

Pronouns

A *pronoun* is a word used in place of a noun, a noun phrase or a noun clause.

Pro- means *in place of* or *in favour of.* Therefore, *pro*noun means *in place of noun* or *in favour of noun.*

As it is with nouns, *pronouns* have their categories or types.

Subject pronouns and object pronouns

A *subject pronoun* is a pronoun used in place of a *subject noun.* It replaces the subject:

1. *James* scolded Lydia.
   He scolded Lydia.

In the first sentence, *James* is the *subject noun (the subject).* In the next one, *he* is the *subject pronoun*; it replaces *James.*

An *object pronoun* is a pronoun used in place of an object noun; it replaces the object:

   1. James scolded *Lydia.*
   James scolded *her.*

Lydia is the *object noun (the object)* in the first sentence. In the next one, *her* is the *object pronoun*, which replaces *Lydia.*

Never mistake *object pronouns* for *subject pronouns.*

Person	Object pronoun	Form	Subject pronoun
1st person	me	Singular	I
1st person	us	Plural	we
2nd person	you	Singular	you
2nd person	you	Plural	you
3rd person	him	Singular	he
3rd person	her	Singular	she
3rd person	it	Singular	it
3rd person	them	Plural	they

The following sentences are wrong:

   1. *Me* goes.
   2. *Her*'s my sister.

The following is the correct way to write the above:

1. *I* am going.
   I go...
2. *She*'s my sister.

These subject and object pronouns fall under *personal pronouns (I, she, it, you, he, they, me, her, him, them, my, his, its, their, us, we, your, and so on).*

Possessive pronouns

A *possessive pronoun* is a pronoun used to replace a possessive noun. Possessive nouns are nouns such as Bob's, Moses', Lydia's, and so on.

An apostrophe (**'**) and an **s** are added to a noun to make it a possessive one: Lydia+**'**+**s**=Lydia**'s**.

When a noun is in a plural form that ends with an **s**, it must not be treated the same way as the above; it must have an apostrophe (**'**) only without an **s**: cows+**'**=cows**'**, not cows**'s**.

Note that *Moses* (singular) has been treated with an apostrophe only without an additional **s**. This is so because the word has many hissing sounds in it. Raymond Murphy, an author, wrote in one of his *English Grammar in Use* apps that only the apostrophe (') is added if the noun contains too many hissing sounds. However, his (Raymond's) way is opposed by other rules that say an apostrophe (') and an **s** are added to any singular noun, even though the noun already ends with an **s**: Charles—Charles**'s**, James—James**'s**, and so on.

Lydia has been treated with an apostrophe (') and an **s** because it does not have any hissing sound.

When a noun is in a plural form that does not end with an **s**, it must be treated with an apostrophe (') and an **s**: people+'+**s**=people**'s**, sheep+' +**s**=sheep**'s**, and so on.

This is how possessive nouns are formed. They express possession: Moses' car (the car belongs to Moses), Lydia's dress (the dress belongs to Lydia), and so on. These are the nouns that *possessive pronouns* replace.

See the following:

1. That car is *Moses'*.
That car is *his*.

In the first sentence, *Moses'* is a possessive noun. In the next one, *his* is a *possessive pronoun* replacing *Moses'*.

The following's set mainly to give you *possessive pronouns*:

Person	Form	Possessive noun	Possessive pronoun	Possessive determiner
1st person	Singular		mine	my
1st person	Plural		ours	our
2nd person	Singular		yours	your
2nd person	Plural		yours	your
3rd person	Singular	Moses'	his	his
3rd person	Singular	Lydia's	hers	her
3rd person	Singular	dog's	its	its
3rd person	Plural	people's	theirs	their
3rd person	Plural	animals'	theirs	their
3rd person	Plural	boys'/girls'	theirs	their
3rd person	Plural	dogs'	theirs	their

When we replace the *possessive nouns* that come before the things they possess, we replace them with *possessive determiners (her, their, our, my, your, and so on)*, not with *possessive pronouns (hers, theirs, ours, mine, yours, and so on)*:

1. Is this *Lydia's dress?*
   Is this *her dress?* [Correct]
   Is this *hers dress?* [Wrong]
2. Is this *dress Lydia's?*
   Is this *dress hers?* [Correct]

Is this *dress her*? [Wrong]

At primary school, you might have come across the following pattern:

1. This dress belongs to *Lydia*. It is *hers*. [Correct]
2. These books belong to *us*. They are *ours*. [Correct]

Reflexive pronouns

A *reflexive pronoun* (myself, yourself, ourselves, themselves, himself, herself or itself) replaces the subject in the position of the object. This is when the subject has become the sufferer of its own action.

See the following:

1. *Jack* killed *himself.*
2. *We* taught *ourselves* the way to do it.
3. *I* taught *myself* to write books.
4. *The longest snake* bit *itself.*

In number 1, *himself* replaces *Jack*, the subject that has appeared in the position of the object. This means the action (killed) has effect on its own subject. The same applies to 2, 3 and 4.

Emphatic pronouns

An *emphatic pronoun* (myself, yourself, ourselves, themselves, himself, herself or itself) is spelt the same as a reflexive pronoun (myself, yourself, ourselves, themselves, himself, herself or itself). The difference only lies on their roles. Unlike the reflexive pronoun, the emphatic pronoun emphasizes the subject.

See the following:

1. *Jack himself* killed *the snake.*
2. *We ourselves* taught *the boys* the way to do it.
3. *I myself* taught *them* to write books.
4. *The snake itself* bit *its young one.*

In number 1, *himself* is emphasizing *Jack*, the subject, that he did it without the help of another person. In this, *Jack* is not the sufferer of his own action. The sufferer of the action (killed) is the snake, which is the object. The same applies to 2, 3 and 4.

Demonstrative pronouns

Demonstrative pronouns are *this*, *that*, *these* and *those*. They replace nouns. *This* and *that* replace singular nouns. *These* and *those* replace plural nouns.

See the following:

1. I prefer Jimmy's behaviour to the *behaviour* of his friend.
I prefer Jimmy's behaviour to *that* of his friend.
2. Joe's dogs are friendlier than the *dogs* of Mr Court Lee.
Joe's dogs are friendlier than *those* of Mr Court Lee.
3. The lifestyle of long ago is different from the *lifestyle* of today.
The lifestyle of long ago is different from *this* of today.
4. The boys you knew years ago are different from the *boys* you see today.
The boys you knew years ago are different from *these* you see today.

In number 1, *behaviour* is singular. In the next sentence, *that* is also singular and is replacing *behaviour.*

In number 2, *dogs* is plural. In the next sentence, *those* is also plural and is replacing *dogs.*

In number 3, *lifestyle* is singular. In the next

sentence, *this* is also singular and is replacing *lifestyle.*

In number 4, *boys* is plural. In the next sentence, *these* is also plural and is replacing *boys.*

Adjectives

An *adjective* is a modifying word. It modifies a noun or a pronoun: *stout*—a *stout* woman (she is *stout*), *angry*—an *angry* boy (he is *angry*), and so on.

Adjectives add more information about people, places or things. Without them, we cannot know more about anything being spoken of. Let's say Mr A and Mr B are telling us the same story:

> **Mr A**: At midnight, a man broke into an office and stole a bunch of keys.

> **Mr B**: At midnight, a *tall* man broke into *John's* office and stole a *small* bunch of *car* keys.

Mr B has given us more information than that from Mr A. He has used some adjectives—*tall* to describe the man, *John's* to modify the office that it belongs to John, *small* to describe the bunch, and *car* to modify the keys that they are of a car.

Adjectives can come before or after nouns:

    1. That's a *tall man.*
        That *man* is *tall.*

In the first sentence, *tall* is before *man,* the noun. This position (of tall) is known as the *attributive* position.

In the next one, *tall* is after *man.* This position is known as the *predicative* position. In this, the adjective comes after a linking verb.

As with nouns and pronouns, adjectives have their categories or types:

Descriptive adjectives

Descriptive adjectives describe nouns: stout—a stout woman, tall—a tall man, big—a big house, angry—an angry boy, and so on.

Demonstrative adjectives

Demonstrative adjectives are *this, that, these* and *those.* They are spelt the same as demonstrative pronouns (this, that, these and those). The difference only lies on the way they are used.

Demonstrative adjectives always come in the attributive position—before nouns. They can't stand alone without the nouns, but demonstrative *pronouns* always stand alone.

This and *that* are singular, and they modify singular nouns. *These* and *those* are plural, and they modify plural nouns.

See the following:

1. *This boy* is rude.
   That boy over there is also rude.
2. *These flowers* are beautiful.
   Those flowers over there are also beautiful.

When there are no nouns, the demonstratives are not adjectives, but they are pronouns:

1. *This ~~boy~~* is rude. [Pronoun]
   That ~~boy~~ is also rude. [Pronoun]
2. *These ~~flowers~~* are beautiful. [Pronoun]
   Those ~~flowers~~ are also beautiful. [Pronoun]

Possessive adjectives

~ 21 ~

Possessive adjectives are *my, her, his, our, their, your* and *its*. They are also called possessive determiners. Like demonstrative adjectives, possessive adjectives always come in the attributive position—before nouns.

See the following:

1. James took *my shirt.*
2. *Their house* is big.
3. This one is *its food.*

From 1, 2 and 3, the possessive adjectives (my, their, and its) are before the nouns (shirt, house, and food).

Proper adjectives

Proper adjectives are formed from proper nouns.

See the following:

Proper noun	Proper adjective
Zimbabwe	Zimbabwean
China	Chinese
Japan	Japanese
America	American
Britain	British

Their first letters are always in uppercase

(capital letters):

1. This is a *Zimbabwean* boy. [Correct]
   This is a *zimbabwean* boy. [Wrong]
2. Here's an *American* girl. [Correct]
   Here's an *american* girl. [Wrong]
3. This *Chinese* girl is cute. [Correct]
   This *chinese* girl is cute. [Wrong]
4. She's *Chinese*. [Correct]
   She's chinese. [Wrong]

Quantifiers

Quantifiers are words that tell about quantity. These are *much, many, several, few, a few, one, two,* and so on. The words are sometimes used as adjectives.

See the following:

1. I saw *many* soldiers.
2. I saw *one* soldier.
3. I saw *ten* soldiers.
4. There was *much* rain last year.

In number 1, *many* modifies *soldiers* that they were many. In number 4, *much* modifies *rain* that it was much. *Many* is used for countable nouns (soldiers), whereas *much* is used for uncountable nouns (rain).

Practice

1. What is a noun?
2. List five proper nouns and five common nouns.
3. Underline the object of the sentence:
    a. He killed a lion.
    b. Temba bought a bicycle.
4. Underline the subject:
    a. Peter saw John.
    b. Sam and his father killed a big snake.
5. Form possessive nouns from the following:
    a. Cows
    b. Tom
    c. People
    d. James
6. Create four sentences in which you use the possessive nouns you formed in number 5.
7. Write two sentences in which you use reflexive pronouns.
8. Write three sentences in which you use emphatic pronouns.
9. Form proper adjectives from the following:
    a. China
    b. Zimbabwe

c. America

d. Britain

10. In your own sentences, use these quantifiers:

a. many

b. much

c. a few

Chapter two

Verbs

A *verb* is a word that shows action (kill) or state of being (be). There are many verbs: be, look, talk, emphasize, beat, cry, start, lie, go, believe, organize, and so on.

Like other words, verbs have categories or types:

Transitive, intransitive and ambitransitive verbs

Transitive verbs are verbs that take objects *directly*. Without taking the objects, the verbs make no sense.

See the following:

1. Jack *killed* the snake.
2. Jack *killed*.

In number 1, *Jack* is the subject, *killed* is the transitive verb, and *the snake* is the object.

In number 2, *Jack* is the subject, *killed* is the transitive verb, but there isn't the object. Hence, number 2 is incomplete and meaningless.

Intransitive verbs, unlike transitive verbs, take objects *indirectly*. And they still make sense even without the objects.

See the following:

1. The baby *cried* for her.
2. The baby *cried*.

Both the sentences above are complete and meaningful. In number 1, *the baby* is the subject, and *cried* is the intransitive verb. After the verb, there is a preposition (for) preventing it (the verb) from taking the object (her) *directly*.

Although number 2 has no object, it makes sense.

The following sentence is wrong:

1. The baby cried her.

This is wrong because the intransitive verb (cried) has taken the object (her) *directly*.

Ambitransitive verbs are both transitive and intransitive:

1. She *started* it.

2. The rain *started.*

With or without the object, each of the above is correct.

Tenses

There are *three* basic tenses and *four* aspects. The tenses tell about *when* the action occurred, occurs or will occur. The aspects tell about *how* the action occurred, occurs or will occur.

We mix each of the three tenses with the four aspects to get many different tense forms. It's like mixing flour, mealie-meal and rice with different ingredients to get different foods.

The following are the three basic tenses:

1. Present tense
2. Past tense
3. Future tense

The four aspects are these ones:

1. Simple
2. Continuous
3. Perfect
4. Perfect continuous

How do you do it? You just insert each of the

aspects between the two words of the basic tense: present tense—present *simple* tense, present tense—present *continuous* tense, present tense—present *perfect* tense, present tense—present *perfect continuous* tense, and so on.

Table 1.

First word	Aspect	Second word	Result
Present	1. Simple 2. Continuous 3. Perfect 4. Perfect continuous	**Tense**	1. Present **simple** tense 2. Present **continuous** tense 3. Present **perfect** tense 4. Present **perfect continuous** tense

Table 2.

First word	Aspect	Second word	Result
	1. Simple 2. Continuous		1. Past **simple** tense 2. Past

Past	3. Perfect	Tense	**continuous** tense
	4. Perfect continuous		3. Past **perfect** tense
			4. Past **perfect continuous** tense

Table 3

First word	Aspect	Second word	Result
Future	1. Simple 2. Continuous 3. Perfect 4. Perfect continuous	Tense	1. Future **simple** tense 2. Future **continuous** tense 3. Future **perfect** tense 4. Future **perfect continuous** tense

Present *simple* tense

This is when the action happens regularly.

See the following:

1. Tom *visits* his uncle twice a week.
2. They *visit* their uncle twice a week.
3. I *visit* my uncle twice a week.

1. He always *buys* me new clothes.
2. They always *buy* me new clothes.
3. I always *buy* my sister new clothes.

In this, the verb changes according to the form of its subject. When the subject is singular, the verb becomes singular. When it, the subject, is plural, the verb becomes plural, too.

Note that the verb whose subject is *I* takes a *plural* form, although *I* is *singular.*

Present *continuous* tense

This is when the action is happening *continuously* at the present time. In this, the main verb ends with '-ing'.

See this:

1. The baby *is crying.*
2. She *is complaining.*
3. I *am going* to school these days.
4. They *are* always *fixing* it.

Present *perfect* tense

This is when the action has just happened. In this, the main verb takes a past participle form.

Look at this:

1. I *have seen* him this morning.
2. Tom *has seen* him this morning.

Note that *seen* is the past participle of *see*, and *saw* is the past tense.

Present *perfect continuous* tense

This is when the action started in the recent past continues at the present time. In this, the main verb ends with '-ing'.

Look at this:

1. They *have been fixing* it since morning.
2. She *has been fixing* it since morning.

Past *simple* tense

This is when the action happened in the past. In this, regular verbs end with either '-ed' or '-d' (walk—walk*ed*, move—move*d*, and so on).

Irregular verbs, unlike regular verbs, have irregular past forms (write—*wrote*, see—*saw*, quit—*quit*, read—*read*, lead—*led*, eat—*ate*, and so on).

See this:

1. I *moved* it yesterday.
2. I *saw* it yesterday.
3. I always *talked* about it.

Past *continuous* tense

This is when the action was happening *continuously* in the past. In this, the main verb ends with '-ing'.

Look at this:

1. She *was singing*.
2. They *were sharing* jokes.

Past *perfect* tense

This is when the action—in the past—had just happened before another action. In this, the main verb takes a past participle form (eaten).

See this:

1. The dog *had died* when the cat died.
   When the cat died, the dog *had died*.

The dog died first, and the cat died second. We usually use *already* with this type: *had **already** died*—the dog had **already** died when the cat died. In this, *died* is the past participle of die.

Past *perfect continuous* tense

This is when the action—in the past—had been happening before another action. In this, the main verb takes a present participle form (eating).

Look at this:

1. Tom *had been fixing it* before Sam *fixed* it.
   Before Sam *fixed* it, Tom *had been fixing* it.

Tom was the first to *fix* it before Sam *fixed* it. And the tense shows that he, Tom, did not do it once.

Future *simple* tense

This is when the action will happen in the future. In this, the main verb is usually preceded with *will, shall* or *be going to*. After these, the verb is a bare infinitive (eat).

Look at this:

1. Tom *will fix* it next week.
2. She *is going to sell* it.
3. We *are going to buy* it.

4. I *shall tell* you about the price.

5. I *am going to see* my father.

Note that the *present* continuous form sometimes acts as the *future* simple tense: *I am talking to him* tomorrow. *She is coming* next year.

Future *continuous* tense

This is when the action will be happening *continuously* in the future. In this, the main verb ends with '-ing'.

See the following:

1. I *shall be visiting* my uncle.

2. I *am going to be visiting* my uncle.

3. She *will be visiting* her brother.

Note that *be* is after *shall, be going to* and *will*.

Future *perfect* tense

This is when the action started in the past will end in the future. In this, the main verb takes a past participle form (eaten).

See this:

1. By next year, Mazira *will have finished*

his work.

The work was started sometime in the past, and it will end in the future.

Future *perfect continuous* tense

This is when the action started in the past will continue to happen in the future. In this, the main verb ends with '-ing'.

Look at this:

> **1.** The next five years, the villagers *will have been working on* the same problem.

The villagers started working on the problem sometime in the past, and they will continue to work on it the next five years.

Auxiliary verbs and modal verbs

Auxiliary verbs and *modal verbs* are also called *helping verbs*. They help main verbs.

The following table has the auxiliary verbs, the modal verbs and their effects on main verbs. *Go* has been used throughout as the main verb.

Auxiliary verb	Modal verb	Main verb (bare	Effect on the main	Result

		infinitive)	verb	
Have		go	becomes a past participle	gone
Be		go	becomes a present participle	going
	Will	go	remains a bare infinitive	go
	Would	go	remains a bare infinitive	go
	Shall	go	remains a bare infinitive	go
	Should	go	remains a bare infinitive	go
	Must	go	remains a bare infinitive	go
	May	go	remains a bare infinitive	go
	Might	go	remains a bare infinitive	go
	Can	go	remains a bare infinitive	go
	Could	go	remains a bare infinitive	go

Had		go	becomes a past participle	gone
Do		go	remains a bare infinitive	go
Did		go	remains a bare infinitive	go

Note that *have* and *do*, apart from working as auxiliary verbs, also work as main verbs:

1. I *have* ten dollars in my wallet.
2. I *do* handiwork.

Subject-verb agreement

The subject-verb agreement simply means the agreement between the subject and the verb.

The verb must always agree with the subject. When the subject is singular, the verb must be singular, too. When the subject is plural, the verb must be plural, too.

Look at this:

1. *Tom goes* to school every day.
   He goes to school every day.
2. *Tom and Mary go* to school every day.
   They go to school every day.

3. *I go* to school every day.

I goes to school every day. [Wrong]

Note that *I* always takes a plural form. Its verb must also take a plural form.

Adverbs

An *adverb* is a word that modifies a verb, an adjective, or another adverb.

See this:

1. The old man *placed* his stick *diagonally* against the wall.

In this, *diagonally* is the adverb modifying *placed*, the verb. This gives the reader a vision on how the action was carried.

Many adverbs are formed by adding *-y*, *-ily* or *-ly* to some adjectives: possible—possib*ly*, happy—happ*ily*, slow—slow*ly*, and so on.

Apart from the above formation, some adverbs are formed by giving prefixes to certain nouns: bed—*a*bed, side—*a*side, and so on.

Others are formed by adding nothing to their adjectives: yearly (adjective)—yearly (adverb), good—well, and so on.

Like other words, adverbs have their types:

Adverbs of manner

Adverbs of manner are formed from descriptive adjectives: beautiful—*beautifully*, happy—*happily*, wise—*wisely*, and so on.

These adverbs can't work in sentences that don't have main verbs to be modified.

Look at this:

1. She is *wisely*. [Wrong]
2. She is *talking wisely*. [Correct]

Number 1 is wrong because the sentence does not have the main verb to be modified by *wisely*.

Number 2 is correct because the sentence has the main verb, *talking*.

Adverbs of degree

Adverbs of degree (*very*, *so*, *extremely*, *too*, and so on) usually modify some adjectives and other adverbs.

See this:

1. The girl is *very beautiful.*
2. The chameleon moved *very slowly.*

In the first sentence, *very* is modifying *beautiful* (an adjective). In the next one, *very* is modifying *slowly* (an adverb).

Adverbs of time

Adverbs of time (*yesterday, today, tomorrow, nowadays, these days,* and so on) tell about the time the action or something took, takes or will take place.

Look at this:

1. The meeting was *yesterday.*
2. The meeting is *today.*
3. The meeting is *tomorrow.*
4. *These days* I'm studying.

In a nutshell, there are many other types of adverbs.

Practice

1. What is a verb?
2. Write three sentences in which you use transitive verbs.
3. Write one sentence in which you use an

intransitive verb.

4. Which tense is each of these verb phrases?

    a. He *walked* away.

    b. Tom *has seen* it.

    c. Sam *was talking* about it.

    d. They *had talked* about it.

    e. We *have been fixing* it.

    f. I *do* this every day.

    g. She *will let* us know about it tomorrow.

    h. I *shall be visiting* them.

5. What is an adverb?

6. Write three sentences in which you use adverbs of manner.

Chapter three

Punctuation

Punctuation clarifies the meaning of what we write.

Given and discussed below are some of the punctuation marks:

Capital letters

Capital letters are uppercase (or big) letters in the alphabet. They are normally used for starting proper nouns and words that start sentences.

Small letters

Small letters (or lowercase letters) are used for starting common nouns. They are not used for starting proper nouns or words that begin sentences.

Question mark

A question mark (?) ends an interrogative or questioning sentence. Without it, the questioning sentence is regarded as wrong.

See this:

1. Is Mazira a teacher. [Wrong]
   Is Mazira a teacher? [Correct]

Exclamation mark

An exclamation mark (!) ends a sentence that expresses some strong feeling.

Look at this:

1. Hey! Stop there! [Strong feeling]
   Hey, stop there. [No strong feeling]

Comma

A comma (,) is used where there is a pause in a sentence.

The comma has more than one purpose:

Purpose 1 [Conditional sentences]

1. If James sees Mary, he will be happy.

The comma is used to separate a dependent clause from an independent clause.

2. James will be happy if he sees Mary.

Note that there's no comma between *happy* and *if*. This is absolutely correct. When you start with an independent clause like this, don't apply a comma.

Purpose 2 [Relative clauses and appositive nouns]

Commas separate non-restrictive relative clauses or non-restrictive appositive nouns or noun phrases from main clauses.

Examples of relative clauses:

a. who donated this
b. whom I talked to
c. which she bought

Look at how the commas work in this:

1. Edson, who donated this, deserves our thanks.

In this, the commas separate *who donated this* (the non-restrictive relative clause) from *Edson deserves our thanks* (the main clause).

Appositive nouns or noun phrases, those nouns or noun phrases that rename or identify the nouns or the noun phrases they follow, are also separated with commas when they are nonrestrictive as well:

2. Edson, the donor, deserves our thanks.

In this, *the donor* is the appositive noun phrase. You should always remember to use the first and the second comma.

Purpose 3 [Nouns of address]

Commas separate a noun of address from the main clause. A noun of address is that noun mentioned or called, in a direct speech, to draw someone's attention.

See this:

1. *Edson*, follow me.
2. Follow me, *Edson*.
3. Do you know, *Edson*, that I'm a soldier?

From the above, *Edson* is the noun of address. *Do you know that I'm a soldier?* and *follow me* are the main clauses.

Purpose 4 [Separating interjections]

Commas separate interjections. An interjection is a word or a group of words used to express feelings and so on.

Examples of interjections:

a. Hi
b. Umm
c. Wow

The interjection—apart from being treated with a period (full stop), an exclamation mark, and so on—is treated with commas:

1. *Umm,* I've no idea.
2. Mary is beautiful, *eh?*

Umm is separated from *I've no idea. Eh* is separated from *Mary is beautiful.*

Purpose 5 [Separating absolute phrases from independent sentences]

Commas separate absolute phrases from main clauses.

Examples of absolute phrases:

a. A jacket on his shoulder
b. Her hands folded on the table
c. The sun rising in the East

Absolute phrases are not independent sentences, but it's easy to turn them into independent sentences. You just give them finite verbs: a jacket on his shoulder—a jacket *hung* on his shoulder, her hands folded on the table—her hands *were* folded on the table, and so on.

Look at how the commas separate these absolute phrases from main clauses:

1. Tino waited for the bus, *a jacket on his shoulder.*
2. *A jacket on his shoulder,* Tino waited for the bus.
3. Tino, *a jacket on his shoulder,* waited for the bus.

Purpose 6 [Preceding coordinating conjunctions]

Commas precede coordinating conjunctions when they, the coordinating conjunctions, join two independent sentences.

Look at this:

1. The hunter fired several bullets at the animals, *and* they all ran away.
2. The hunter fired several bullets to the animals, *but* he killed none.

Don't place the comma after the coordinating conjunction:

1. The hunter fired several bullets at the animals *and,* they all ran away.
2. The hunter fired several bullets to the animals *but,* he killed none.

Coordinating conjunctions have FAN BOYS as their acronym. This (FAN BOYS) stands for *for, and, nor, but, or, yet* and *so.*

Purpose 7 [The serial / Oxford comma]

As we use commas in a list of elements, the last element—before we write *and*—is either given a comma or not. This comma is called the serial comma or the Oxford comma.

Look at this:

> **1.** I saw a lion, an elephant, a leopard**,** and a zebra.

The comma after leopard is the serial comma or the Oxford comma.

You can also write without the serial comma:

> **2.** I saw a lion, an elephant, a leopard and a zebra. [Correct]

Purpose 8 [Long interrupters]

Commas enclose interrupters, those words or phrases that come in the middle of main sentences.

Look at this:

> **1.** James, *I'm sure*, is a soldier.
> James, *according to the reports I got from those boys yesterday*, is a soldier.

In the first sentence, the interrupter is *I'm sure,* and the main clause is *James is a soldier.* In the next one, the interrupter is *according to the reports I got from those boys yesterday,* and the main clause is the same.

Purpose 9 [Separating dialogue tags from direct speeches]

Commas separate dialogue tags (*she said* and so on) from direct speeches.

See this:

1. She said, "I am fine."
2. "I am fine," she said.
3. "I am fine," she said, "but my brother is not."

Purpose 10 [Introductory phrases]

Commas separate introductory phrases from main clauses.

Look at this:

1. *After his friend,* Jack took the bike.

After his friend is the introductory phrase. *Jack took the bike* is the main clause.

Full stop (period)

A full stop (.) ends a complete sentence that is not a question or that does not have an expression of strong feeling.

Look at this:

1. Tom visited his uncle.
2. Go to school.
3. I will tell you.

Apart from ending complete sentences, full stops (periods) are also used to mark abbreviations: Z.R.P., Z.B.C., and so on.

Inverted commas

Quotation marks (inverted commas / quotes / quotations) are used to quote a direct speech or a peculiar word or phrase. There are double quotations (" ") and single quotations (' ').

See this:

1. She said, "I am fine."
   She said, 'I am fine.'
2. I saw "MVURAYATOTA" written on the wall.
   I saw 'MVURAYATOTA' written on the wall.

In the first sentence, the quotation marks quote a direct speech. In the second one, they (the quotations) quote a peculiar word.

Apostrophe

An apostrophe (') has a shape similar to that of a closing inverted comma ('), but they're not the same.

The apostrophe is used to form possessive nouns:

1. Edson+'+s=Edson's
2. James+'=James' (James's)

The apostrophe is also used to replace missing letters:

1. Do not = **don~~o~~t** = don't
2. Has not = **hasn~~o~~t** = hasn't
3. Are not = **aren~~o~~t** = aren't
4. You are = **you~~a~~re** = you're
5. You would = **you~~would~~** = you'd
6. I will = **I~~will~~** = I'll

Questions

A question starts with either *where, what, why, who, whose, whom, which* or *how*.

See this:

1. *Where* is Tom?
2. *What* do you want?
3. *Why* are you sad?
4. *Whose* car is this?
5. *Whom* should I talk to?
6. *Who* took it?
7. *Which* is yours?
8. *How* do you open it?

Sometimes, a question starts with a helping verb:

1. *Do* you know him?
2. *Did* you see it?
3. *Have* you fixed it?
4. *Must* we leave just like that?
5. *Has* he said it that way?
6. *Are* we strangers?
7. *Is* she your friend?
8. *Am* I allowed to get it?

Sometimes, we leave out the helping verbs and use ordinary statements as questions:

1. You know him?
2. You saw it?
3. You fixed it?
4. We leave just like that?

5. He said it that way?
6. We are strangers?
7. She is your friend?
8. I am allowed to get it?

A preposition also can start a question:

1. *To* whom shall I give my advice?
2. *Under* whose authority are you doing it?

Tag questions

A tag question is a question with a combination of a statement and a question tag.

See this:

1. Mazira is a teacher, isn't he?
2. Mazira is not a teacher, is he?

Tag questions have types. In this type, when the statement (Mazira is a teacher.) is positive, the tag (isn't he?) is negative. When the statement (Mazira is not a teacher.) is negative, the tag (is he?) is positive.

The *echo tag*, the other type, is different. In this, when the statement is positive, the tag also is positive. When the statement is negative, the tag is also negative.

Look at this:

> **Edson**: I did it!
> **Peter**: *You did, did you?*
> **Edson**: Yes!

Peter used the echo tag to answer Edson. He could even use it without the statement:

> **Edson**: I did it!
> **Peter**: *Did you?*
> **Edson**: Yes!

Echo questions

An echo question is a certain type of a question to a statement or to another question. It comes as an answer.

Look at this:

> **Edson**: I did it!
> **Peter**: *Did you?*

> **Tom**: Edson's lying.
> **Peter**: *He's what?*

> **Edson**: Tom, did you tell Peter I'm a liar?
> **Peter**: *Did I tell him that?*

In this, Peter's answers are echo questions.

Answers to questions

Answers to questions may be positive or negative.

Look at this:

> **Mary**: Do you know Edson?
> **Joe**: Yes, I do (know him).

> **Mary**: Do you know Edson?
> **Jack**: No, I don't (know him).

> **Mary**: Do you know Edson?
> **Joe**: Yes.

> **Mary**: Do you know Edson?
> **Jack**: No.

There are so many ways of giving answers to questions. Your teacher can help you with some more.

Double negatives in answers

Be careful not to write double negatives in answers:

Mike: Do you know anything about it?
Sam: No, I *don't* know *nothing* about it.

Mike: Do you know anything about it?
John: No, I *don't* know anything about it.
[Correct]

There are double negatives (*don't* and *nothing*) in Sam's answer. The answer vaguely means Sam *knows anything* because there is *nothing* he *doesn't* know.

Vowel letters and consonant letters

Vowel letters (vowels) and consonant letters (consonants) are letters in the alphabet: Aa, Bb, Cc, Dd, Ee, Ff, Gg, Hh, Ii, Jj, Kk, Ll, Mm, Nn, Oo, Pp, Qq, Rr, Ss, Tt, Uu, Vv, Ww, Xx, Yy and Zz.

Vowels

Vowels are Aa, Ee, Ii, Oo and Uu.

Consonants

Consonants are Bb, Cc, Dd, Ff, Gg, Hh, Jj, Kk, Ll, Mm, Nn, Pp, Qq, Rr, Ss, Tt, Vv, Ww, Xx, Yy and Zz

Every English word is formed from the alphabet.

Using 'a'

The word 'a' is known as an indefinite article. It is used before a singular noun (of countable things) starting with a consonant sound.

Look at this:

1. I bought *a car*.

The noun 'car' starts with a letter 'c' that has a consonant sound, so 'a' is used before the noun.

2. They need *a university* in their town.

The noun 'university' starts with a vowel 'u', but the vowel has a consonant sound (*yu*), so 'a' is used before the noun.

Using 'an'

The word 'an' is known as an indefinite article. It is used before a singular noun (of countable things) starting with a vowel sound.

Look at this:

1. I bought *an egg*.

The noun 'egg' starts with a letter 'e' that has a vowel sound, so 'an' is used before the noun.

2. I need *an hour*.

The noun 'hour' starts with a consonant 'h', but the consonant is silent; it has no sound. Hence, we pick the sound from the next letter. In this case, the next letter 'o' is a vowel, and it has a vowel sound, so 'an' is used before the noun.

Using 'the'

The word 'the' is known as the definite article. It is used before any noun that has been mentioned before. It is also used before a noun of any specific thing, place or person.

See this:

Passage 1

> Out of the blue, *a* strange *boy* appeared in front of us. *The boy* was in *a* dirty *overall. The overall* was tattered. When he saw *a police officer* with me, he ran away. *The police officer* ran after him.

Passage 2

The headmaster of my school always wants to chat with *the* president of this country, but he, *the* president, is always busy.

In passage 1, every noun before which 'the' has been used has been mentioned before.

In passage 2, every noun before which 'the' has been used is specific.

Indefinite articles before modifiers

Sometimes there are modifiers (*adjectives* and so on) between indefinite articles and nouns. In this case, you consider first the noun if it deserves the article. Second, you consider whether the first modifier starts with a consonant sound or a vowel sound. (**1**) If the noun is singular and countable, it deserves the article. (**2**) If the modifier starts with a consonant sound, it deserves 'a', but if it starts with a vowel sound, it needs 'an'.

Look at this:

1. I saw *a m*ulti-colored *egg.*
2. *An e*gg-shaped *ball* is not for soccer.

In number 1, we considered using an indefinite article because the noun 'egg' is singular and countable. After that, we considered using 'a' because the modifier (multi-colored) starts with a consonant sound.

Zero article

Zero article means no article. Uncountable nouns and plural countable nouns take no articles when they are mentioned for the first time. This is when they are not specific. When they are specific, they take the definite article 'the'.

Look at this:

1. *Sugar* is sweet.
2. I saw multi-colored *eggs*.
3. Egg-shaped *balls* are not for soccer.
4. *Dogs* are domestic animals.

The following ones are *specific*:

1. Use *the sugar* on the table.
2. I saw *the multi-colored eggs* you talked about.
3. Who brought *the egg-shaped balls*?
4. *The dogs* are for sale.

5. *The president* of my country is a generous man.

Direct speech and indirect (reported) speech

A direct speech lies within quotations. When the speech is changed to an indirect (reported) speech, it does not lie within the quotations. In this case, pronouns, verbs and other things change.

Look at this:

1. Tinashe says, "I will talk to Peter."
Tinashe said (that) he would talk to Peter.

2. She said, "They have seen me."
She said (that) they had seen her.

3. I said, "I am happy."
I said (that) I was happy.

4. "We are going to build it for them," they promised.
They promised (that) they were going to build it for them.

In indirect speeches, 'that' is sometimes left out.

This table shows the changes that occur:

Direct speech	Word type	Indirect (reported) speech
I	subject pronoun	he/she
me	object pronoun	him/her
my	Possessive determiner	his/her
mine	possessive pronoun	his/hers
we	subject pronoun	they
us	object pronoun	them/us
our	possessive determiner	their
ours	possessive pronoun	theirs
you	subject pronoun	he/she/I/we/they
you	object pronoun	him/her/me/us/them
your	possessive determiner	his/her/my/our/their
yours	possessive pronoun	his/hers/mine/ours/theirs
eat	main verb	ate
can	modal verb	could
will	modal verb	would
shall	modal verb	should
may	modal verb	might

must	modal verb	must
do	auxiliary / main verb	did
is/are/am	auxiliary verb	was/were/was
myself	reflexive / emphatic pronoun	himself/herself
ourselves	reflexive / emphatic pronoun	themselves
here	adverb/noun	there

Note that the table has not given you everything.

Practice

1. Punctuate this:

are you one of those rude boys asked his teacher

no i am not he said if you think im lying to you you can ask mark he knows me very well

2. Use a preposition to start a question.

3. Rewrite this paragraph and use articles:

Out of the blue, strange boy appeared in front of us. Boy was in dirty overall. Overall was tattered. When he saw police officer with me, he ran away. Police officer ran after him.

4. Change each of the following to a reported speech:

    a. We asked, "Where are the boys?"

    b. "I'm not one of them," he said to the police officer. "If you doubt me, ask Mary."

    c. "I can do it myself," I told them.

    d. He promised, "I will be visiting you every month."

Chapter four

Comparative

A comparative is used where two things, animals or persons are compared.

Look at this:

1. Tinotenda is *younger* than Patson.
2. She is *more beautiful* than her sister.

Incompatible comparative

This is when the comparative is made comparing things that have no common features.

Look at this:

1. The *particles* of sand are larger than *clay*.

This comparative is illogical; it doesn't make sense. You can't compare the *particles* with the *clay*; instead, you compare them with the other *particles*.

Compatible comparative

This is when the comparative is made comparing things that have common features.

See this:

1. The *particles* of sand are larger than the *particles* of clay.
   The *particles* of sand are larger than *those* of clay.

This comparative is logical; it makes sense.

Superlative

A superlative is used where *more than two* things, animals or persons are compared.

Look at this:

1. Tinotenda is the *youngest* of the *three* boys.
2. Of *all* the girls in this village, Thandiwe is the *most* beautiful girl.

Incompatible superlative

As it is in the comparative, there is also the possibility of making incompatible superlatives.

Look at this:

1. Mr Chikwira's *herd* of cattle is the largest of all the *villagers*.

This superlative is illogical; it doesn't make sense. You can't compare the *herd* (cattle) with the *villagers* (people).

Compatible superlative

This is when the superlative is made comparing things with the same features.

See this:

1. Mr Chikwira's *herd* of cattle is the largest of all the *herds* in the village.
   Mr Chikwira's *herd* of cattle is the largest of all the villagers' (*herds*).

This superlative is logical; it makes sense.

Double comparative and double superlative forms

Be careful not to make double comparative or superlative forms.

Look at this:

1. John is *more happier* than Sipho.
   John is *happier* than Sipho. [Correct]

2. Mr Kabiseni is the *most richest* man in

this village.

Mr Kabiseni is the *richest* man in this village. [Correct]

Practice

1. Correct the following sentences:
   a. She is bad than he is.
   b. Thandiwe is more beautiful of the three girls.
   c. My clothes are more beautiful than Mary.
   d. This is the most richest man.

Chapter five

Syntax

This is the arrangement of words and phrases to create well-formed sentences. [*Concise Oxford Dictionary—Tenth Edition*]

Sentences consist of words from different classes that must work together to make sense.

The following are some things to consider when creating grammatical sentences:

Prepositions

A preposition is a word that expresses a relationship between the object and the rest of the sentence. It usually comes before the object.

Look at this:

1. Those children were going *to school.*
2. The ball is *under the table.*
3. The boy stood *near the bull.*
4. The birds flew *over the mountain.*
5. She hid *behind a bush.*

Sometimes, the preposition comes after an

interrogative sentence:

1. Whom shall we communicate *with*?
2. Where's the guy you did it *for*?

The preposition comes also in front of the question:

1. *With* whom shall we communicate?
2. *For* what reason are you doing it?

Repetition

Avoid repeating the same subject or object.

Look at this:

Passage 1

> *The teacher* entered the classroom, *he* walked towards his table, *he* took a piece of chalk and *he* wrote some work on the board. *The pupils* wrote the work and *they* gave it to him.

There is the repetition of the subject in the above.

Passage 2

> *The teacher* entered the classroom,

walked towards his table, took a piece of chalk and wrote some work on the board. *The pupils* wrote the work and gave it to him.

The repetition of the subject has been avoided in this.

Either *and* or

Either works with *or*. When two subjects are joined with them (*either* and *or*), the verb agrees with the subject near it (the verb).

Look at this:

1. Either Patson or *I am* going to do it.
Either I or *Patson is* going to do it.

2. Either the boys or the *girls are* coming tomorrow.

3. Either the boy or the *girls are* coming tomorrow.
Either the girls or the *boy is* coming tomorrow.

Neither *and* nor

Neither works with *nor*. When two subjects are

joined with them (*neither* and *nor*), the verb agrees with the subject near it (the verb).

Look at this:

1. Neither Patson nor *I am* going to do it.
   Neither I nor *Patson is* going to do it.

2. Neither the boys nor the *girls are* coming tomorrow.

3. Neither the boy nor the *girls are* coming tomorrow.
   Neither the girls nor the *boy is* coming tomorrow.

Not only *and* but also

Not only works with *but also*. When two subjects are joined with them (*not only* and *but also*), the verb agrees with the subject near it (the verb).

See this:

1. Not only the boys but the *girl* also *is* coming tomorrow.
   Not only the girl but the *boys* also *are* coming tomorrow.

Both *and* and

Both works with *and*. When two subjects are joined with them (*both* and *and*), the verb is always plural.

Look at this:

> **1.** Both the *girl* and the *boy are* my children.

Note that these subjects must have the same singular or plural form. You can't use *both* in the following:

> **1.** *Both* the girl and the boys are my children. [Wrong]
> *Both* the boys and the girl are my children.

In the next sentence, *both* is correct only if it means both of the boys. This means the person is talking about three children (two boys and one girl).

So *and* that

So works with *that*.

See this:

1. The sun was *so* hot *that* our cattle hid in the shade.
2. We were *so* late *that* we hired a taxi.

In this, 'that' is sometimes left out:

1. The sun was *so* hot our cattle hid in the shade.
2. We were *so* late we hired a taxi.

In the same manner, 'so' is sometimes left out:

1. The sun was hot *that* our cattle hid in the shade.
2. We were late *that* we hired a taxi.

In any case, never regard as wrong the following words when they are used alone without their partners: *either, neither* and *both*.

Look at this:

1. *Either* of these methods *is* good.
2. *Neither* of the teachers *has* mentioned it.
3. *Both* (of) the boys *are* my children.

Note that the verbs are singular in numbers 1 and 2.

Modifying phrases and clauses

A modifying phrase or clause is a group of words used to describe or modify a noun, a pronoun, a verb, and so on.

The following are modifying phrases and clauses:

a. relative clauses
b. prepositional phrase
c. participle relative clauses
d. adjective phrase
e. adverbial phrase

a. Relative clauses

A relative clause modifies a noun.

Look at this:

1. Edson, *who donated this*, deserves our thanks.
2. The house *that Tom talked about* belongs to Mr Mazira.
3. I know the man *whose car is red*.

From the above, the clauses in *italics* are the relative clauses. In numbers 1 and 2, the relative clauses modify the subjects. In number 3, the relative clause modifies the object.

There are restrictive and non-restrictive relative clauses. Restrictive relative clauses have no *commas* around them: The house *that Tom talked about* belongs to Mr Mazira. Non-restrictive relative clauses have *commas* around them: Edson, *who donated this,* deserves our thanks.

Sometimes, the relative pronouns in the objective case (*whom, that* and *which*) are left out:

1. The house *that Tom talked about* belongs to Mr Mazira.
   The house *Tom talked about* belongs to Mr Mazira.

2. The man *whom they showed us* is a writer.
   The man *they showed us* is a writer.

3. The foods *which we donate to them* need to be examined first.
   The foods *we donate to them* need to be examined first.

b. Prepositional phrase

A prepositional phrase begins with a

preposition: *on* the table, *under* the table, and so on. The prepositional phrase modifies a noun, a pronoun or a verb.

Look at this:

1. Use the sugar *on the table.*
2. The cat *under the table* is not ours.

The prepositional phrase 'on the table' modifies the noun 'sugar' that the sugar is on the table. In number 2, 'under the table' modifies the noun 'cat' that the cat is under the table.

Look at the phrases when they modify verbs:

1. I hid *in a cave.*
2. The cat sat *under the table.*

In number 1, the prepositional phrase 'in a cave' modifies the verb 'hid'. In number 2, 'under the table' modifies the verb 'sat'.

c. Participle relative clauses

Participle relative clauses (*talking to you, seen around your home*, and so on) are derived from relative clauses: The man (*who is*) *talking to you* needs help. The boy (*who was*) *seen around your home yesterday* stole shoes from your neighbour.

Look at this:

1. The man *talking to you* needs help.
2. The boy *seen around your home yesterday* stole shoes from your neighbour.

In the above, the participle relative clauses modify the subjects.

d. Adjective phrase

An adjective phrase is a group of words that modifies a noun or a pronoun.

Look at this:

1. A cup *full of milk* fell down from the table.
2. The cup was *full of milk*.

From the above, the adjective phrase 'full of milk' modifies the noun 'cup'.

e. Adverbial phrase

An adverbial phrase is a phrase that modifies a verb, an adjective or another adverb.

See this:

1. I walked *up the hill.*
2. Jack ran *up and down the road.*

From the above, the adverbial phrases (*up the hill* and *up and down the road*) modify the verbs (*walked* and *ran*).

Misplaced modifiers

Be careful not to misplace modifying phrases or clauses. Misplaced modifiers cause some confusion.

Look at this:

1. The dog got on the bus *with its owner.*
2. The dog *with its owner* got on the bus.
3. The man killed a goat *in an overall.*

The first two sentences seem to have different meanings. Number 1 seems to mean that the dog got on the bus and that the bus was with its owner.

Number 2 means the dog with its owner (the owner of the dog) got on the bus.

Number 3 is funny. It says a goat was wearing an overall. It needs to be written as follows:

3. The man *in an overall* killed a goat.

Now, it makes sense. The man was wearing an overall.

Noun phrases

When a noun is surrounded with modifiers, it becomes a noun phrase: man—*the man in an overall*, group—*a group of words*, and so on. In this case, the verb agrees with the head noun being modified. The other noun or nouns in the modifier have nothing to do with the verb.

Look at this:

1. *The 'people' on the bus 'are' afraid of the dog.*
2. *The 'elephant' feeding on tree leaves 'is' friendly.*
3. *The 'house' that Tom, Mary and Peter talked about 'belongs' to Mr Mazira.*

The verb always agrees with the head noun, the main noun being modified.

Noun clauses

A noun clause is a clause introduced by *that, what, whether, how, where,* and so on. When the noun clause is the subject, the verb is singular.

Look at this:

1. *That he killed three lions* is a lie.
2. *Where they want to go* is not known.
3. *Whether those people were robbers* is something else.
4. *How I will communicate with my friends* remains my secret.
5. *What you are doing* is disgusting.
6. *How the donkeys, the cows, the hens and the dogs were killed* is sad.

Note that every verb after the *italicized* noun clause is singular.

Negative phrases in front of sentences

When negative phrases come in front of a sentence, the subject and the auxiliary or the modal verb swap positions.

Look at this:

1. *'I shall'* **never** let her go away.
   Never *'shall I'* let her go away.

2. *Under no circumstances will they* allow you to participate in their group.
3. *Seldom do the birds* fly north.

Practice

1. List any two modifying phrases or clauses and use them in your own sentences.
2. Correct the following sentences:
    a. The man killed a goat in a black suit.
    b. The boy in a nest shot a bird.
3. Choose the correct verb:
    a. The people on the bus, who were near the man with a dog, (was/were) afraid.
    b. The game that Peter, Sam, Mary, Tom and Mark played (were/was) not easy.
    c. That all the boys (is/are) stubborn is a lie.
    d. How those people were murdered by the robbers (remain/remains) an important thing to remember.
4. Use your own words to complete the following declarative sentences:
    a. Seldom...
    b. Never...
    c. I was telling Joe about the robbers; little ... know he was one of them.

Chapter six

Answers

Note that some of the answers in this section just serve as examples.

Chapter one

1. A noun is a naming word.
2. Five proper nouns—*Zimbabwe, Joe, Mary, Edson* and *Mazira.*
   Five common nouns—*car, boy, sky, sugar* and *love.*
3. The object of the sentence—
   a. He killed <u>a lion</u>.
   b. Temba bought <u>a bicycle</u>.
4. The subject of the sentence—
   a. <u>Peter</u> saw John.
   b. <u>Sam and his father</u> killed a big snake.
5. Possessive nouns—
   a. Cows'
   b. Tom's
   c. People's
   d. James' (James's)
6. Four sentences with the possessive nouns in number 5—
   a. I saw the *cows'* calves behind that hill.
   b. Is this *Tom's* dog?

    c. My *people's* houses have thatched roofs.

    d. *James' (James's)* toys were broken by Tom.

7. Two sentences with reflexive pronouns—
The boy hurt *himself.*
She did it for *herself.*

8. Three sentences with emphatic pronouns—
She did it *herself.*
I *myself* built the house.
We did it *ourselves.*

9. Proper adjectives formed from *China, Zimbabwe, America* and *Britain*—

    a. Chinese

    b. Zimbabwean

    c. American

    d. British

10. Sentences with *many, much* and *a few*—

    a. I saw *many* soldiers.

    b. I need *much* sand to fill in the pit.

    c. *A few* people were in the room.

Chapter two

1. A verb is a word that shows action or state of being.

2. Three sentences with transitive verbs—
The boy *killed* three birds.

He *stole* shoes.

I *bought* a pen.

3. One sentence with an intransitive verb—
   The baby *cried* for her mother.

4. The tense of each of the verb phrases—
   a. *Past simple tense* (He *walked* away).
   b. *Present perfect tense* (Tom *has seen* it).
   c. *Past continuous tense* (Sam *was talking* about it).
   d. *Past perfect tense* (They *had talked* about it).
   e. *Present perfect continuous tense* (We *have been fixing* it).
   f. *Present simple tense* (I *do* this every day).
   g. *Future simple tense* (She *will let* us know about it tomorrow).
   h. *Future continuous tense* (I *shall be visiting* them).

5. An adverb is a word that modifies a verb, an adjective or another adverb.

6. Three sentences with adverbs of manner—
   The tortoise moved *slowly* across the road.
   Angrily, the girl explained to them how she had been treated.

They laughed *hysterically*.

Chapter three

1. The correct punctuation—

"Are you one of those rude boys?" asked his teacher.

"No, I am not," he said. "If you think I'm lying to you, you can ask Mark. He knows me very well."

'Are you one of those rude boys?' asked his teacher.

'No, I am not,' he said. 'If you think I'm lying to you, you can ask Mark. He knows me very well.'

2. *To* whom must I give this?

3. The correct way of using articles—

Out of the blue, *a* strange boy appeared in front of us. *The* boy was in *a* dirty overall. *The* overall was tattered. When he saw *a* police officer with me, he ran away. *The* police officer ran after him.

4. Reported speech—

a. We asked to know where the boys were.

b. He said to the police officer that he was not one of them and told him to ask Mary if he doubted him.

   c. I told them that I could do it myself.

   d. He promised that he would be visiting them (or us) every month.

Chapter four

1. The correct sentences—

   a. She is *worse* than he is.

   b. Thandiwe is *the most beautiful* of the three girls.

   c. My clothes are more beautiful than *Mary's* (clothes).

   d. This is *the richest* man.

Chapter five

1. Two modifying phrases or clauses—

- prepositional phrase—
  Use the sugar *on the table*.
- relative clause—
  Edson, *who donated this*, deserves our thanks.

2. The correct sentences—

   a. The man *in a black suit* killed a goat.

   b. The boy shot a bird *in a nest*.

3. The correct verb—

   a. The people on the bus, who were near the man with a dog, *were* afraid.

b. The game that Peter, Sam, Mary, Tom and Mark played *was* not easy.

c. That all the boys *are* stubborn is a lie.

d. How those people were murdered by the robbers *remains* an important thing to remember.

4. Sentences starting with negative phrases—

a. Seldom *does this dog bark at people.*

b. Never *shall I allow them to use it.*

c. I was telling Joe about the robbers; little *did I* know he was one of them.

Citation

1. Eastwood, J. (1994). *Oxford Guide to English Grammar.* New York: Oxford University Press.
2. Herring, P. (2016). *Complete English Grammar Rules.* Dublin, Ireland: Farlex International Ltd.

Index